delicious.
Sizzle

Welcome

Since the dawn of time, when humans first learnt to use fire and heat, our taste buds have been tantalised by the sound and smell of food sizzling over a hot flame.

Whether you are a beginner cook or a budding Masterchef there will be something in *Sizzle* to inspire you – from decadent main meals, to quick and simple brunches and tasty midweek suppers.

Drawing on flavours from many cuisines and at the same time offering stress-free cooking, this is a book full of recipes that we know you will love and that are sure to impress. If you are ready to be tempted, light that fire, pop a pan over the heat and let's get things sizzling.

Beef and Veal

6   Beef on lemongrass skewers with cucumber salad
8   Vitello tonnato burgers
10   Steak with simple bearnaise
12   Bulgogi with easy pickle
14   Moorish beef skewers with cauliflower couscous
16   Mexican steak sandwich
18   Pepper steak burger
20   Cevapi
22   New World curried sausages
24   Eye fillet with raspberry sauce
26   Green tea yakitori with Japanese seasoned rice

Lamb

28   Lamb cutlets with spiced vegetable chips
30   Rosemary lamb kebabs with lemon & olive relish
32   It's a lamb wrap
34   Herb-rubbed lamb cutlets with pea & feta salad
36   Lamb & preserved lemon meatballs with crushed broad bean salad
38   Zaatar-crusted lamb with chickpea & bean salad
40   Hot and fiery hummus

Seafood

42   Salmon skewers with fennel & orange salad
44   Barbecued prawn cocktails
46   Pan-fried fish with malt vinegar tartare
48   Tea 'smoked' salmon
50   Tuna wasabi burgers
52   Greek salad with calamari
54   Tuna with green tea noodles and black vinegar dressing
56   Scallops with cauliflower skordalia and curry dressing
58   Mexican corn cakes with avocado and prawns
60   Chermoula fish with tahini sauce
62   Spicy swordfish with avocado & lime salsa
64   Crumbed whiting with citrus salad
66   Spicy garlic prawns cooked in beer
68   Salmon with tomato & coconut sambal
70   Fried squid with lime & ginger mayo

Poultry

72   Mexican chicken with smoky tomato salsa
74   Tunisian spiced chicken with hummus and pomegranate
76   Quail under a brick with Asian gremolata
78   Barbecue tapas
80   Wasabi crumbed chicken
82   Panko-crumbed chicken Caesar salad
84   Oregano chicken on bean & olive salad
86   Quail with rose petals and yoghurt
88   Spicy chicken with spoon salad

Pork

90   Pork cutlets with peach pan chutney

92   Sausage saltimbocca

94   Spanish eggs

96   Spanish pork with orange & poppyseed salad

98   Pea pancakes with crisp pancetta and
       sweet chilli sauce

100   Vineyard sausages

102   Sausages with red cabbage and onion jam

104   Fried eggs with bacon jam

106   XO pork stir-fry with Asian greens

Vegetarian

108   Grilled zucchini wraps

110   Haloumi with Mediterranean salad

112   Beet burgers

114   Asparagus bruschetta with poached eggs
       and pecorino

116   Eggplant pesto timballos

118   Asparagus with crumbed haloumi

120   Spinach gnudi with sage burnt butter

122   Crispy polenta with truffled mushrooms
       and Taleggio

124   Strawberry & brie sandwiches

Beef on lemongrass skewers with cucumber salad

4 x 200g beef eye fillets
3 lemongrass stems
Sunflower oil, to brush

Marinade
¼ cup (60ml) peanut oil
½ red onion, chopped
2 garlic cloves, chopped
2 tbs chopped coriander
2 kaffir lime leaves*,
   thinly sliced
2 tsp ground turmeric
1 tsp ground cumin
2 tbs soy sauce
1 tsp palm sugar*
1 tbs lime juice

Cucumber salad
3 Lebanese cucumbers
¼ cup (65g) palm sugar*
¼ cup (60ml) lime juice,
   plus extra wedges to serve
2 small red chillies, seeds
   removed, finely chopped
4 eschalots, thinly sliced
1 tbs fish sauce
¼ cup (35g) roasted
   peanuts, chopped

For the marinade, place all the ingredients in a mini food processor and whiz until a smooth paste. Transfer to a bowl. Cut the beef into 4cm chunks, then coat well in the marinade. Cover and refrigerate for 1 hour.

Meanwhile, for the cucumber salad, slice the cucumbers into thin strips, place in a sieve and sprinkle with salt. Leave over the sink for 20 minutes to drain, then rinse and pat dry with paper towel. Combine palm sugar, lime juice, chilli, eschalot and fish sauce in a bowl, stirring until the sugar has dissolved. Season to taste and set aside.

Cut the lemongrass into 15cm lengths. Thread the beef onto the lemongrass skewers and bring to room temperature.

Preheat a chargrill pan or barbecue to medium-high heat.

Brush the chargrill pan or barbecue hotplate with oil and cook the skewers, turning, for 4–5 minutes until lightly charred on the outside, but still rare in the centre. Remove the beef skewers from the heat and allow to rest, loosely covered with foil, for 5 minutes.

Toss the cucumber with the palm sugar dressing and stir through the peanuts. Serve the skewers with the cucumber salad. **Serves 4**

* Kaffir lime leaves and palm sugar are available from Asian food shops.

Vitello tonnato burgers

800g veal mince
1 small onion, finely chopped
1 garlic clove, finely chopped
¼ cup (65g) capers in brine,
    rinsed, drained, chopped,
    plus 2 tbs whole capers
¼ cup (40g) chopped
    black olives
Finely grated zest of 1 lemon
¼ cup finely chopped
    flat-leaf parsley leaves
1 tbs olive oil, plus extra
    to brush
4 burger buns, split, toasted
Salad leaves, sliced tomatoes
    and lemon wedges,
    to serve

Tonnato sauce
185g can tuna in oil, drained
1 cup (300g) whole-egg
    mayonnaise
1 tbs capers, rinsed, drained
2 tsp grated lemon zest,
    plus 1 tbs lemon juice
1–2 anchovy fillets in oil
    (optional), drained

Place the veal mince, onion, garlic, chopped capers, olives, lemon zest and parsley in a bowl. Season, then mix well to combine. Shape into four thick burger patties and chill for 1 hour to firm up.

Meanwhile, heat the olive oil in a frypan over medium-high heat. Cook the whole capers for 1 minute or until crisp. Set aside.

For the tonnato sauce, place all the ingredients in a blender and whiz to a smooth sauce. Set aside.

Preheat a barbecue or chargrill pan over high heat.

Brush the burger patties with a little oil and grill for 2–3 minutes each side until cooked through.

Spread some tonnato sauce on the bun bases, then top with the salad leaves, burger patties, more tonnato sauce, fried capers and tomato. Sandwich with the bun tops and serve with lemon wedges.
Serves 4

Steak with simple bearnaise

2 tbs tarragon vinegar*
   or white wine vinegar
1 eschalot, finely chopped
6 black peppercorns
2 tbs chopped tarragon
   leaves*
4 rib-eye steaks
2 tbs olive oil, to brush
3 egg yolks
140g unsalted butter
Watercress or rocket leaves,
   to serve
Shoestring fries, to serve

Place the vinegar, eschalot, peppercorns, half the tarragon leaves and 2 tablespoons water in a pan over medium heat and simmer for 1 minute until reduced to about 1 tablespoon of liquid. Strain through a fine sieve, pressing down on solids.

Brush the steaks with oil and season with salt and pepper. Heat a chargrill pan over high heat and cook the steaks for 3–4 minutes each side for medium-rare (or until cooked to your liking). Rest in a warm place, loosely covered with foil, for 5 minutes.

Meanwhile, place egg yolks and tarragon reduction in a blender and whiz to combine. Melt butter in a pan over medium-low heat. With the motor running, very slowly and carefully pour the butter through the feed tube of the blender while it's still hot and bubbling, to form a thick sauce. Stir in remaining tarragon. Drizzle sauce over steak, season and serve with watercress and fries. **Serves 4**

* Tarragon vinegar is available from delis and gourmet food shops. Fresh tarragon is available from selected greengrocers.

Bulgogi with easy pickle

300g beef fillet steak

100ml soy sauce

1 small onion, grated

1 tsp sesame oil

2 tsp finely grated ginger

2 tbs brown sugar

3 garlic cloves, finely
   chopped

2 butter lettuces,
   leaves separated

Steamed jasmine rice,
   shredded spring onion
   and thinly sliced chillies,
   to serve

Pickled vegetables

90g caster sugar

⅔ cup (185ml) rice vinegar

1 carrot, cut into thin
   matchsticks

½ daikon*, peeled, cut
   into thin matchsticks

Enclose the beef in plastic wrap, then freeze for 1 hour (this will make it easier to slice).

Combine the soy sauce, onion, sesame oil, ginger, brown sugar and garlic in a bowl. Using a sharp knife, very thinly slice the beef, then add to the marinade. Cover and chill for at least 2 hours.

Meanwhile, for the pickled vegetables, place the caster sugar, vinegar, 100ml water and a good pinch of salt in a saucepan over medium-low heat, stirring until the sugar dissolves. Remove from the heat, then add the vegetables and stand for 2 hours to pickle.

Preheat a barbecue or chargrill pan over high heat.

Drain the beef, discarding the marinade. In batches if necessary, cook the beef for 10 seconds each side or until charred.

Divide the lettuce among plates and top with the rice, beef, spring onion and chilli. Drain the pickled vegetables and serve with the bulgogi. **Serves 4–6**

* Daikon is available from greengrocers and Asian food shops.

Moorish beef skewers with cauliflower couscous

2 tbs cumin

1 tbs sweet paprika

½ tsp smoked paprika
   (pimenton)

1 tsp nutmeg

1 tsp turmeric

½ tsp cayenne

½ cup flat-leaf parsley, finely
   chopped

2 garlic cloves,
   finely chopped

½ cup (125ml) Pedro
   Ximénez* or other
   sweet sherry

⅓ cup (80ml) extra virgin
   olive oil

1.2kg beef rump,
   cut into 4cm pieces

1 lemon, thickly sliced

Cauliflower couscous

¾ cup (150g) couscous

200g cauliflower florets

2 tbs extra virgin olive oil

¼ cup (40g) dried cranberries

2 tbs pistachios

¼ cup finely chopped flat-leaf
   parsley

Combine spices, parsley, garlic, sherry and olive oil in a large, non-reactive glass or ceramic bowl. Add beef and turn to coat. Cover and marinate in the fridge for 4 hours.

Soak 8 bamboo skewers in cold water for 30 minutes (or use 8 metal skewers).

Meanwhile, to make cauliflower couscous, place couscous in a bowl and pour over ¾ cup (185ml) warm water. Cover with a tea towel and set aside. Cook cauliflower in boiling salted water for 3 minutes or until just tender (don't overcook). Drain and refresh under cold running water. Dry well on paper towel, then place in a food processor and pulse to the consistency of breadcrumbs. Fluff couscous with a fork, season with sea salt and freshly ground black pepper, then stir through cauliflower, olive oil, cranberries, pistachios and parsley.

Drain beef and thread onto skewers. Heat a chargrill pan or barbecue to high. Cook the beef, turning and brushing occasionally with marinade, for 3–4 minutes until medium-rare or until cooked to your liking. Cook the lemon slices for 1–2 minutes each side until lightly charred.

Serve beef skewers with cauliflower couscous and chargrilled lemon slices. **Serves 4**

* Pedro Ximénez is an intense, sweet Spanish sherry available from selected bottle shops; substitute sweet sherry.

Mexican steak sandwich

1 garlic clove, finely chopped

¼ tsp paprika

½ tsp ground cumin

½ tsp dried oregano

1 tsp lime juice

100ml olive oil

2 x 180g scotch fillet or sirloin
steaks, halved to give 4 thin
steaks

3 spring onions, thinly sliced

1 bunch coriander, leaves
picked

2 fresh jalapenos* or other
long green chillies, seeds
removed, chopped

4 vine-ripened tomatoes,
chopped

2 tbs red wine vinegar

4 long crusty bread rolls,
split, toasted

Good-quality shop-bought
guacamole, to serve

Combine the garlic, paprika, cumin, oregano, lime juice,
1 tablespoon olive oil and some salt and pepper in a bowl.
Add the steaks and turn to coat in the mixture. Cover and marinate
in the fridge for 2–3 hours.

Place the spring onion, coriander (reserving some leaves for
garnish), chilli, tomato, vinegar and remaining olive oil in a bowl.
Season well, then stir to combine. Set salsa aside.

Heat a chargrill pan or barbecue on high heat. Cook the steaks
for 1 minute each side until charred. Remove and rest, loosely
covered, for 2 minutes.

Spread the toasted rolls with guacamole, top with steaks, spoon
over salsa, then garnish with coriander leaves and serve with
Mexican beer. **Makes 4**

* Jalapenos are available from selected greengrocers and farmers'
markets.

Pepper steak burger

800g beef mince
1 onion, finely chopped
1 egg, lightly beaten
¼ cup chopped flat-leaf
    parsley leaves
1 tbs olive oil
2 tbs green peppercorns in
    brine, drained, lightly
    crushed with a fork
2 tbs brandy
1 tsp Dijon mustard
150ml thickened cream
4 slices sourdough,
    chargrilled, rubbed with
    a halved garlic clove

Preheat the oven to 170°C.

Place beef, onion, egg and 2 tablespoons parsley in a bowl, season, then mix well with your hands. Using damp hands, form into 4 thick patties. Cover and chill for 10 minutes.

Heat the oil in a frypan over medium heat. Cook the patties for 2 minutes each side until sealed. Transfer to a baking tray, then bake for 5 minutes or until cooked through.

Meanwhile, drain the excess fat from the pan. Add the peppercorns, brandy, mustard and cream to the pan, then simmer over medium-low heat, stirring, for 2–3 minutes until slightly thickened. Season with sea salt, then stir in the remaining tablespoon of chopped parsley.

Place a piece of grilled sourdough on each plate, top with burger patties, drizzle with the pepper sauce and serve. **Serves 4**

Cevapi

500g lean beef mince
100g lean lamb mince
250g lean pork mince
3 garlic cloves, finely
    chopped
1 tbs bicarbonate of soda
2 tbs paprika
Olive oil, to rub and drizzle
Ajvar relish*, sour cream
    and rocket leaves, to serve

Place the mince, garlic, bicarbonate of soda and paprika in a food processor, season with 2 teaspoons sea salt and lots of black pepper, then pulse to just combine.

Using damp hands, form the mixture into 10 sausage shapes, then chill in the fridge for at least 10 minutes to firm up.

Heat a chargrill pan, frypan or barbecue hotplate over medium-high heat. Rub the cevapi with a little oil and cook, turning, for 3–5 minutes until browned and cooked through. Serve with ajvar relish and sour cream. Sprinkle with black pepper, scatter with rocket leaves and drizzle with a little extra olive oil. **Makes 10**

* Ajvar relish is made from roasted red capsicums, garlic and eggplant. It is available from delis and gourmet food shops.

New World curried sausages

1 tbs olive oil

12 fresh curry leaves*,
   plus extra to fry

1 tsp panch phoran*

1 small onion, thinly sliced

½ long green chilli, seeds
   removed, finely chopped

2 garlic cloves,
   finely chopped

2 tsp grated ginger

1 tsp sweet paprika

½ tsp curry powder

400g can chopped tomatoes

1 tsp caster sugar

1 tsp tamarind puree*

400g can chickpeas,
   rinsed, drained

1 tbs chopped coriander

12 thin pork or beef sausages

Mashed potato, to serve

To make curry sauce, heat oil in a frypan over medium heat. Add curry leaves and panch phoran, then cook, stirring, for 1 minute or until fragrant. Add onion and cook until softened but not coloured. Add chilli, garlic and ginger, then cook for a further 1 minute. Add paprika and curry powder, then cook for a further minute. Add tomato, sugar and tamarind, then cook, stirring occasionally, for 10–15 minutes until thickened and the oil starts to separate. Add 1 cup (250ml) water and bring to a simmer, then add chickpeas and coriander, and simmer for a further 5 minutes.

Meanwhile, cook sausages in a frypan over medium-high heat, turning, until browned and cooked through. In the same pan, fry extra curry leaves until crisp, then drain on paper towel.

Serve sausages with mash, sauce and fried curry leaves. **Serves 4**

* Curry leaves are available fresh from selected greengrocers and dried from supermarkets. Panch phoran is an Indian spice blend that includes cumin, fenugreek and fennel; available from spice shops, Indian food shops and online at herbies.com.au; substitute brown mustard seeds. Tamarind puree or paste is available from selected supermarkets and Asian food shops.

Eye fillet with raspberry sauce

1 tbs olive oil

10g unsalted butter

4 x 180g beef eye fillet steaks

1 cup (250ml) red wine

2 tbs caster sugar

250g raspberries

1 cup (250ml) good-quality
   beef stock

3 tbs creme fraiche or sour
   cream

Potato mash and steamed
   green beans, to serve

Place the oil and butter in a frypan over high heat. Season the steaks with salt and pepper and cook for 2–3 minutes each side until browned and cooked to medium-rare, or until done to your liking. Transfer to a plate, cover loosely with foil and set aside while you make the sauce.

Return the pan to medium heat and add the red wine, sugar and most of the raspberries (reserving about ½ cup to garnish). Cook, stirring, for 2–3 minutes until the fruit has broken down. Add the stock and cook for 3–4 minutes until syrupy. Whisk in the creme fraiche or sour cream and season to taste. Strain the sauce, discarding the solids, and return to the pan. Add any beef resting juices and the reserved berries to the pan and stir until heated through.

Serve the steaks on potato mash and green beans, drizzled with the raspberry sauce. **Serves 4**

Green tea yakitori with Japanese seasoned rice

⅓ cup (80ml) light soy sauce

2 tbs sweet chilli sauce

2 lemongrass stems (inner core only), grated

1 tsp chilli oil*

2 tsp loose-leaf green tea

1cm piece ginger, grated

2 tbs chopped coriander leaves

600g beef fillet steak, cut into 3cm pieces

1½ cups (300g) jasmine rice

¼ cup Japanese furikake seasoning*

Pickled ginger* and mizuna*, to serve

Place the soy sauce, sweet chilli sauce, lemongrass, chilli oil, green tea, ginger and coriander in a large bowl. Add beef, stirring to coat, then place in the fridge to marinate for at least 4 hours or overnight.

Place 12 small wooden skewers in a bowl of cold water and allow to soak for 1 hour.

Cook the rice according to the packet instructions.

Meanwhile, preheat a barbecue or chargrill pan over medium-high heat.

Drain the beef, then thread onto the soaked skewers. Cook the beef, turning, for 3–4 minutes for rare or until cooked to your liking.

Toss the rice with the furikake seasoning. Serve the beef skewers with seasoned rice, pickled ginger and mizuna. **Serves 4**

* Chilli oil, Japanese furikake seasoning, pickled ginger and mizuna are available from Asian food shops and selected supermarkets.

Lamb cutlets with spiced vegetable chips

2 tbs olive oil, plus extra
   to deep-fry
2 tbs lemon juice
2 garlic cloves, finely
   chopped
2 tsp dried oregano
12 French-trimmed lamb
   cutlets
1 tbs cumin seeds
1 tsp smoked paprika
   (pimenton)
1 kumara, peeled
1 parsnip, peeled
1 beetroot, peeled

Combine olive oil, lemon juice, garlic and oregano in a large dish. Add lamb cutlets and turn to coat in the mixture, then cover and marinate in the fridge for 30 minutes.

Meanwhile, toast the cumin seeds in a dry frypan for 30 seconds or until fragrant. Place cumin in a mortar or spice grinder with the smoked paprika and ½ teaspoon peppercorns, crush to a powder, then stir in 2 teaspoons sea salt.

Slice the kumara and parsnip about 1mm thick (a mandoline is ideal), then slice the beetroot last and keep separate to prevent it from staining the other vegetables.

Preheat a lightly oiled chargrill pan or barbecue on high heat. In batches, grill the lamb for 2–3 minutes each side until lightly charred but still pink in the middle, or cooked to your liking. Cover with foil, then keep warm in a low oven.

Meanwhile, heat the oil in a deep-fryer or large saucepan to 190°C (a cube of bread will turn golden in 30 seconds when the oil is hot enough). Leaving the beetroot until last, cook the vegetables in batches for 1–2 minutes until crisp and golden. Drain on paper towel. Toss the vegetables in the seasoned salt and serve with the cutlets.
Serves 4–6

Rosemary lamb kebabs with lemon & olive relish

4 rosemary branches, plus
   1 tbs rosemary leaves,
   chopped
2 garlic cloves, finely
   chopped
2 tbs olive oil
1 tbs paprika, plus extra
   to dust
1 tbs lemon juice
500g lamb fillet, cut into
   2cm cubes
4 vine-ripened tomatoes,
   seeds removed, chopped
1 tbs chopped preserved
   lemon rind* (white pith and
   flesh discarded)
2 tbs chopped pitted
   kalamata olives
2 tbs chopped flat-leaf
   parsley
Thick Greek-style yoghurt,
   to serve

Soak 4 rosemary branches or bamboo skewers in cold water for 30 minutes to prevent them from burning.

Combine the garlic, oil, rosemary leaves, paprika and lemon juice in a glass or ceramic dish. Season well, then add the lamb, tossing to coat well. Cover and marinate in the fridge for 1–2 hours.

Meanwhile, combine the tomato, preserved lemon rind, olives and parsley in a bowl. Season to taste (it will already be quite salty from the lemon), then set the relish aside.

Thread the lamb onto the branches or skewers. Heat a chargrill pan or barbecue on medium-high heat. Cook the lamb, turning occasionally, for 6–8 minutes until browned all over but still juicy in the centre. Serve the skewers with the relish and yoghurt, dusted with a little extra paprika. **Serves 4**

* Preserved lemons are available from gourmet food shops and delis.

It's a lamb wrap

2 tbs extra virgin olive oil

2 tbs chopped oregano

2 garlic cloves, finely
chopped

2 x 250g lamb backstraps,
trimmed

4 spring onions, thinly sliced
on the diagonal

120g marinated feta, drained,
crumbled

⅓ cup (50g) pitted kalamata
olives, roughly chopped

2 preserved lemon quarters*,
white pith removed, rind
thinly sliced

¼ cup (60g) semi-dried
tomatoes, chopped

1 cup mint leaves

100g rocket

4 slices of mountain bread*

Combine the oil, oregano and garlic in a bowl. Coat the lamb in
the marinade, cover and stand for 30 minutes.

Preheat the oven to 190°C.

Heat an ovenproof frypan over medium-high heat. Season the
lamb, then cook for 2 minutes each side to seal. Transfer to the
oven and bake for 5 minutes for medium-rare. Remove from the
oven and rest, loosely covered with foil, for 5 minutes.

Thinly slice the lamb, then place in a bowl with the spring onion,
feta, olives, preserved lemon rind, semi-dried tomato and mint and
gently toss to combine.

Place rocket on the mountain bread, top with the lamb and feta
salad, then roll up and serve. **Makes 4**

* Preserved lemons are available from selected supermarkets,
gourmet food shops and delis. Mountain bread is available from
supermarkets.

Herb-rubbed lamb cutlets with pea & feta salad

1 tbs whole black
   peppercorns
2 garlic cloves
2 long red chillies, seeds
   removed, finely chopped
2 tbs thyme leaves
2 tbs chopped sage leaves
2 tbs chopped
   flat-leaf parsley
¾ cup (185ml) olive oil
12 French-trimmed
   lamb cutlets
1 tsp Dijon mustard
1 tsp honey
Finely grated zest
   and juice of 1 lemon

Pea & feta salad
250g small snow peas,
   trimmed
250g sugar snap peas,
   trimmed
200g frozen baby peas
2 cups mint leaves
200g marinated feta,
   drained

Place peppercorns, garlic, half the chilli and 1 teaspoon salt in a mortar and pestle and pound until coarsely ground. Add herbs and pound into a coarse paste. Stir in ¼ cup (60ml) olive oil and transfer to a large bowl. Add the lamb, turning to coat well in the herb marinade. Cover, then stand at room temperature for 30 minutes.

Preheat a chargrill pan or barbecue to medium-high heat.

Cook the lamb for 2–3 minutes each side for medium-rare or until cooked to your liking. Rest, loosely covered with foil, for 5 minutes.

Meanwhile, for the pea and feta salad, blanch the snow peas, sugar snap peas and baby peas in boiling salted water for 3 minutes or until just tender. Drain, then refresh in cold water. Transfer to a serving platter and top with mint leaves and feta.

Combine mustard, honey, lemon zest and juice, and remaining chilli, then slowly whisk in remaining ½ cup (125ml) olive oil. Season.

Arrange the lamb cutlets on top of the pea and feta salad, drizzle with the honey dressing and serve. **Serves 4**

Lamb & preserved lemon meatballs with crushed broad bean salad

½ cup (35g) fresh
   breadcrumbs
¼ cup (60ml) milk
500g lamb mince
1 garlic clove, finely chopped
½ cup (40g) grated parmesan
2 tbs finely chopped
   preserved lemon rind*
½ cup finely chopped mint
   leaves, plus extra leaves to
   serve
500g podded fresh or frozen
   broad beans
1 tsp lemon zest
2 tbs olive oil
Warm flatbreads, watercress
   sprigs, Greek-style yoghurt
   and lemon wedges, to
   serve

Combine breadcrumbs and milk in a bowl. Set aside for 5 minutes.

Place lamb, garlic, parmesan, preserved lemon and half the chopped mint in a bowl. Season well with sea salt and freshly ground black pepper, then add breadcrumb mixture and combine well. Roll lamb mixture into 3cm balls and place on a plate. Cover and refrigerate for 30 minutes to firm up.

Cook fresh broad beans in a saucepan of boiling salted water for 3 minutes or blanch frozen broad beans for 1 minute. Drain, refresh in iced water, then remove outer pods. Place beans in a bowl with lemon zest, 1 tablespoon oil and remaining ¼ cup chopped mint. Season, then roughly crush beans with a fork.

Heat remaining 1 tablespoon oil in a large frypan over medium-high heat. Cook meatballs, turning, for 4–5 minutes until browned all over and cooked through.

Serve meatballs with flatbread, broad bean salad, watercress, yoghurt, lemon wedges and extra mint leaves. **Serves 4**

* Preserved lemons are available from gourmet food shops and delis.

Zaatar-crusted lamb with chickpea & bean salad

4 x 150g lamb backstraps
¼ cup (60ml) olive oil
¼ cup (30g) zaatar (Middle
    Eastern spice blend)*
300g green beans, trimmed
400g can chickpeas, rinsed,
    drained
1 cup mint leaves, torn

Tahini dressing
½ cup (140g) tahini*
3 garlic cloves, crushed
Juice of 1 lemon
Pinch of cayenne pepper
Pinch of ground coriander
Pinch of ground cardamom

Rub the lamb with 2 tablespoons olive oil, then coat in the zaatar. Season, then set aside while you prepare the dressing and salad.

For the dressing, place all the ingredients in a blender and whiz to combine. With the motor running, slowly add ½ cup (125ml) warm water until you have a smooth dressing. Season and set aside.

Blanch the beans in boiling salted water for 2 minutes or until just tender. Drain, then refresh in iced water. Place the refreshed beans in a bowl with the chickpeas and mint.

Heat remaining 1 tablespoon oil in a frypan over medium-high heat and cook the lamb for 3 minutes each side for medium-rare or until cooked to your liking. Rest, loosely covered with foil, for 5 minutes.

Lightly toss half the tahini dressing with the salad. Thickly slice the lamb, then serve with the salad and remaining tahini dressing.
Serves 4

* Zaatar and tahini are available from delis and Middle Eastern food shops.

Hot and fiery hummus

½ cup (125ml) extra virgin
   olive oil, plus 1 tbs to
   pan-fry
1 tsp dried chilli flakes
2 x 440g cans chickpeas,
   rinsed, drained
¾ cup (75g) toasted walnuts
2 garlic cloves
2 tsp ground cumin
Juice of 1 lemon
1 red onion, finely chopped
150g lamb mince
1 tsp sumac*
2 tbs chopped coriander,
   plus extra leaves to garnish
Seeds of ½ pomegranate*
   (optional)
Flatbreads, to serve

The day before you want to make the hummus, place the oil and chilli in a small pan and cook gently over low heat for 2–3 minutes, then stand overnight to infuse.

The following day, set aside ⅓ cup chickpeas. Place the remainder in a food processor with the walnuts, garlic, 1 teaspoon cumin, half the lemon juice and half the chilli oil. Process until smooth, then season. Taste the hummus and adjust the balance with lemon juice; you may also need to add a little warm water to achieve a soft, smooth consistency. Set aside the hummus while you prepare the lamb.

Heat 1 tablespoon oil in a frypan over medium heat, then add the onion and cook, stirring, for 3–4 minutes until soft. Add the lamb and remaining garlic and cook, stirring, for 6–8 minutes until the lamb is brown. Add the sumac and remaining cumin, season well, then stir in the chopped coriander.

When ready to serve, spread the hummus on a plate, then scatter with the lamb, pomegranate seeds and the reserved chickpeas. Garnish with the coriander leaves, and serve with flatbreads.
Serves 4

* Sumac is a lemon-flavoured Middle Eastern spice made from ground dried berries, available from supermarkets and Middle Eastern shops. Pomegranates are available in season from greengrocers.

Salmon skewers with fennel & orange salad

4 x 120g skinless salmon
   fillets, cut into 2cm cubes
2 limes (skin on), cut into
   2cm cubes
1 fennel bulb, very thinly
   sliced (a mandoline is
   ideal), plus fennel fronds
   to garnish
2 oranges, peeled, sliced into
   5mm rounds, plus strips of
   zest to garnish
1 small red onion, thinly
   sliced

Dressing
½ cup (125ml) olive oil
2 tbs white wine vinegar
Juice of 1 large lime
2 tbs chopped flat-leaf
   parsley

Soak 8 bamboo skewers in cold water for 30 minutes.

Preheat a chargrill pan or barbecue to medium-high.

For the dressing, place the ingredients in a screwtop jar with some salt and pepper, and shake to combine. Taste and adjust seasoning if necessary. Set half the dressing aside.

Place the salmon in a bowl and pour over the dressing, turning to coat in the mixture. Thread alternating pieces of salmon and lime onto the skewers, then grill or barbecue for 2–3 minutes, turning, until lightly charred and just cooked through.

Arrange the fennel, orange and onion in 4 bowls. Dress the salads with the remaining dressing, then top with the salmon skewers. Garnish with fennel fronds and orange zest, then serve. **Serves 4**

Barbecued prawn cocktails

½ iceberg lettuce, leaves torn

1 avocado, sliced

1 mango, cut into 1cm cubes

12 large green prawns,
 peeled (tails intact)

2 tsp olive oil

1 tbs finely chopped chives

Cocktail sauce

⅓ cup (100g) mayonnaise

2 tbs tomato sauce

1 tbs thickened cream

1 tbs Worcestershire sauce

Juice of ½ lemon

For the cocktail sauce, combine the mayonnaise, tomato sauce, cream, Worcestershire sauce and lemon juice in a small bowl. Season with sea salt and black pepper.

Divide the lettuce among 4 dishes, then add the avocado and mango and drizzle with a little cocktail sauce.

Heat a chargrill pan or barbecue to high. Brush the prawns with the oil and season well with sea salt and freshly ground black pepper. Chargrill the prawns for 1–2 minutes each side until lightly charred and cooked through.

Arrange 3 prawns on top of each salad. Drizzle with extra dressing and sprinkle with chopped chives. **Serves 4**

Pan-fried fish with malt vinegar tartare

2 tbs olive oil

8 boneless white fish fillets with skin (such as coral trout)

½ cup (150g) whole-egg mayonnaise

3 tbs thickened cream

⅓ cup (80ml) malt vinegar, plus extra to serve

1 tbs finely chopped cornichons (small pickled cucumbers)

1 tbs chopped fresh tarragon leaves*

1 tbs finely chopped flat-leaf parsley, plus extra to garnish

Oven-baked chips, to serve

Heat the oil in a large non-stick frypan over medium heat. Season the fish, add to the pan and cook for 2 minutes each side or until the skin is crispy and fish is cooked through.

Set aside in a warm place while you make the sauce.

Drain most of the oil from the pan. Add the mayonnaise, cream, vinegar and cornichon, and stir for 1–2 minutes to warm through. Remove from the heat, then stir in the tarragon and parsley.

Divide the fish and chips among plates, then drizzle with the tartare sauce. Season with salt and pepper, garnish with parsley, and serve with extra malt vinegar for the chips. **Serves 4**

* Fresh tarragon is available from selected greengrocers.

Tea 'smoked' salmon

2 lapsang souchong teabags*
1 garlic clove, finely chopped
5cm piece ginger, grated
⅓ cup (80ml) kecap manis
    (Indonesian sweet soy
    sauce)*
1 tbs honey
1 tbs sesame oil
4 salmon fillets with skin
1 tbs olive oil
Jasmine rice and steamed
    Asian greens, to serve

Place the teabags in a jug, pour over 200ml boiling water, and leave for 5 minutes to infuse. Press the teabags against the side of the jug to extract maximum flavour, then discard. Add the garlic, ginger, kecap manis, honey and half the sesame oil and stir until combined, then allow to cool. Place the salmon in a glass or ceramic dish and pour over the marinade, then cover and marinate in the fridge for at least 4 hours or overnight.

Remove the salmon from the marinade, reserving ½ cup (125ml), and pat dry with paper towel. Heat the remaining sesame oil and olive oil in a frypan over medium-high heat and cook the salmon, skin-side down for 2 minutes, then turn and cook for 2 minutes (or until done to your liking).

Meanwhile, bring the reserved marinade to a gentle simmer over medium-low heat (don't allow to boil). Serve the salmon on rice with Asian greens, drizzled with the sauce. **Serves 4**

* Lapsang souchong teabags are available from selected supermarkets. Kecap manis is available from Asian food shops.

Tuna wasabi burgers

500g skinless tuna fillet,
  pin-boned, chopped
2 spring onions, finely
  chopped
1 tbs sesame seeds
2 tbs fresh breadcrumbs
2 tbs soy sauce
2 garlic cloves, finely
  chopped
2 tsp finely grated ginger
½ cup coriander leaves
1 small red chilli, seeds
  removed, finely chopped
2 tsp cornflour
1½ tsp wasabi paste
1 tbs olive oil
½ cup (150g) whole-egg
  mayonnaise
4 burger buns, split, toasted

Pickled vegetables
1 small red chilli, seeds
  removed, finely chopped
1 tbs mirin
1 tbs light soy sauce
2 tsp caster sugar
2 tsp rice wine vinegar
½ telegraph cucumber
2 small carrots

Place the tuna, spring onion, sesame seeds, breadcrumbs, soy sauce, garlic, ginger, coriander, chilli, cornflour and ½ teaspoon wasabi in a food processor and pulse a few times until just combined, being careful not to over-process. Divide the mixture into 4 portions, then use damp hands to form into burgers. Cover and refrigerate for 30 minutes.

Meanwhile, for the pickled vegetables, combine the chilli, mirin, soy sauce, sugar and rice wine vinegar in a bowl, stirring to dissolve the sugar. Using a vegetable peeler, cut the cucumber and carrot into long thin ribbons. Toss with the dressing and stand for 10 minutes.

Preheat a chargrill pan or barbecue to medium-high heat.

Brush the chargrill pan or barbecue hotplate with the oil. Cook the burgers for 5 minutes each side or until the outside is charred, but the centre is still pink.

Combine the mayonnaise with the remaining 1 teaspoon wasabi, season and set aside.

Serve the burgers and toasted buns with the mayonnaise and pickled vegetables. **Serves 4**

Greek salad with calamari

2 mini cos lettuces,
    leaves separated
250g cherry tomatoes, halved
1 telegraph cucumber,
    cut into 2cm pieces
½ cup (75g) pitted kalamata
    olives
2 cups (340g) polenta
2 tbs finely chopped flat-leaf
    parsley
1 cup (250ml) buttermilk
500g squid tubes, cleaned,
    sliced into rings
3 cups (750ml) peanut oil,
    to deep-fry
125g feta, crumbled

Vinaigrette
4 tbs extra virgin olive oil
2 tbs lemon juice
½ tsp Dijon mustard
½ tsp sugar
salt and pepper, to taste

Place lettuce, tomato, cucumber and olives in a bowl.

Combine polenta and parsley in a bowl. Place buttermilk in a bowl and season with sea salt and freshly ground black pepper. Dip calamari first into buttermilk, allowing excess to drain back into bowl, then coat in polenta mixture, gently shaking off excess.

Heat oil in a deep-fryer or large saucepan to 180°C (a cube of bread will turn golden in 35 seconds when the oil is hot enough) and cook calamari, in batches, until crisp and golden.

To make vinaigrette, whisk together all ingredients in a bowl.

Toss salad with ¼ cup vinaigrette dressing, scatter over feta and serve with calamari. **Serves 4**

tuna with green tea noodles and black vinegar dressing

400g centre-cut
   sashimi-grade tuna*
200g green tea noodles*
2 cups (300g) frozen, podded
   edamame beans (young
   green soy beans)*
1 bunch coriander,
   leaves picked
Black sesame seeds*,
   to serve

Black vinegar dressing
¾ cup (180ml) mirin
   (Japanese rice wine)*
150ml yellow bean sauce*
   or light soy sauce
⅓ cup (80ml) black vinegar*
⅓ cup (75g) caster sugar
2 tbs grated ginger
4 garlic cloves, finely
   chopped
3 small red chillies, seeds
   removed, very finely
   chopped
1 tsp sesame oil

For the black vinegar dressing, combine the mirin, yellow bean sauce, black vinegar and caster sugar in a saucepan with 150ml cold water. Place over medium heat, stirring until sugar has dissolved. Add the ginger, garlic and chilli, then simmer for 5 minutes or until slightly reduced. Stir in the sesame oil, then set aside to cool.

Cut the tuna into 3cm cubes and toss with half the cooled dressing. Cover and allow to marinate in the fridge for 30 minutes.

Meanwhile, soak 8 wooden skewers in cold water for 30 minutes.

Cook the green tea noodles according to the packet instructions, adding the edamame for the final 1 minute of cooking time. Drain, refresh in cold water and set aside.

Preheat a chargrill pan or barbecue to medium-high heat.

Thread the tuna onto the soaked skewers. Grill the tuna for 2 minutes each side or until lightly charred on the outside, but still pink in the centre.

Toss the noodles and edamame with the coriander leaves and remaining dressing, then divide among bowls. Top with tuna skewers, sprinkle with black sesame seeds and serve. **Serves 4**

* Sashimi-grade tuna is available from fishmongers. Green tea noodles, edamame beans, black sesame seeds, mirin, yellow bean sauce and black vinegar are available from Asian food shops.

Scallops with cauliflower skordalia and curry dressing

350g cauliflower
300ml extra virgin olive oil,
    plus extra to drizzle
200g Dutch cream potatoes
2 cups (500ml) milk
6 garlic cloves
Grated zest of ½ lemon,
    plus 2 tbs lemon juice
12 scallops without roe
1 cup micro herbs* or
    coriander leaves

Curry dressing
150ml extra virgin olive oil
2 eschalots, finely chopped
2 tsp korma curry paste
50ml lemon juice

For the dressing, heat 1 tablespoon oil in a small frypan over medium heat. Add the eschalot and cook, stirring, for 1–2 minutes until softened. Add curry paste, stir for a few seconds until fragrant, then place in a small processor and process with ¼ cup (60ml) olive oil (or stir together in a bowl). Transfer to a bowl, stir in remaining oil and lemon juice, then season to taste. For a smooth dressing, pass through a sieve, pressing down on solids. This dressing can be made up to 1 day in advance.

Preheat oven to 180°C. Break cauliflower into small florets. Toss half the florets in 1 tablespoon oil and season to taste. Spread on a baking tray and roast for 20 minutes.

Meanwhile, cut potatoes into pieces the same size as the cauliflower florets, then place in a pan with the milk, garlic and remaining florets. Simmer over medium-low heat for 8–10 minutes until tender, then drain, reserving liquid. Pass potato and cauliflower through a ricer or mouli into a bowl. Stir in lemon zest and juice, remaining olive oil and enough cooking liquid to make a smooth puree. Season skordalia and keep warm.

Season the scallops and drizzle with oil. Heat a frypan or chargrill pan over medium heat. In batches, cook the scallops for 30 seconds each side until golden but still slightly translucent in the centre.

Spread some of the skordalia on each plate, top with the scallops, then scatter with the roast cauliflower, sprinkle with micro herbs and drizzle with the curry oil. **Serves 4**

* Micro herbs are available from select greengrocers and farmers' markets.

Mexican corn cakes with avocado and prawns

2 avocados, chopped

2 tbs lime juice, plus
  lime wedges to serve

2 tbs sour cream

½ cup chopped coriander
  leaves, plus extra
  coriander leaves to serve

2 tsp ground cumin

2 jalapeno chillies*, seeds
  removed, chopped,
  plus extra sliced jalapeno
  chilli to serve

1 cup (150g) plain flour

1 tsp baking powder

1 tbs caster sugar

2 eggs

½ cup (125ml) milk

2 cups (320g) corn kernels
  (from about 3 corn cobs)

½ cup thinly sliced
  spring onion

2 tbs olive oil

20 cooked prawns, peeled
  (tails intact), deveined

Place the avocado, lime juice, sour cream, ¼ cup coriander, 1 teaspoon cumin and half the chilli in a food processor and whiz to a coarse paste. Set aside.

Sift the flour and baking powder into a bowl. Add the sugar, remaining 1 teaspoon cumin and a pinch of salt.

Place the eggs and milk in a separate bowl and lightly whisk to combine. Add the milk mixture to the flour mixture, whisking until you have a smooth, stiff batter. Add corn, spring onion and remaining chilli and chopped coriander. Season, then stir to combine.

Place the oil in a non-stick frypan over medium-high heat. In batches, drop 2 tablespoons batter into the frypan for each corn cake and cook for 1–2 minutes each side until golden and cooked through. Drain on paper towel and keep warm while you cook the remaining corn cakes.

Divide the corn cakes among plates, then top with avocado puree, prawns, sliced jalapeno and extra coriander. Serve with lime wedges. **Serves 4**

* Jalapenos are available from selected greengrocers and farmers' markets.

Chermoula fish with tahini sauce

1 tsp cumin seeds

1 tsp coriander seeds

1 tsp smoked paprika
   (pimenton)

¼ tsp dried chilli flakes

1 tbs finely grated ginger

2 tsp ground turmeric

2 garlic cloves, roughly
   chopped

2 cups flat-leaf parsley leaves

2 cups coriander leaves

Finely grated zest of
   2 lemons, plus juice of
   4 lemons

4 x 200g skinless barramundi
   fillets or other firm
   white fish

½ cup (140g) tahini*

Olive oil, to brush

Rocket leaves and mint
   leaves, to serve

Place the cumin and coriander seeds in a small frypan over medium heat. Cook, stirring, for 1 minute until fragrant. Transfer to a mini food processor with the smoked paprika, chilli flakes, ginger, turmeric, garlic, parsley, coriander leaves, zest and juice of 2 lemons and 1 teaspoon salt. Whiz until a thick paste. Coat the fish in the chermoula marinade and set aside for 15 minutes.

Meanwhile, combine the juice of the remaining 2 lemons with the tahini and ½ cup (125ml) water and season. Set aside.

Preheat a chargrill pan or barbecue to medium-high heat.

Brush the chargrill pan or barbecue with oil and cook the fish for 3–4 minutes each side until cooked through. Transfer to serving plates, drizzle with the tahini sauce and serve with rocket and mint leaves. **Serves 4**

* Tahini is available from health food shops and selected supermarkets.

Spicy swordfish with avocado & lime salsa

1 lime, plus 2 tbs lime juice
  and wedges to serve
1 avocado, flesh cut into
  1cm cubes
1 Lebanese cucumber,
  peeled, halved lengthways,
  seeds removed, cut into
  1cm cubes
½ small red onion, finely
  chopped
1–2 long red chillies (to taste),
  seeds removed, finely
  chopped
1 cup coriander leaves
¼ cup (60ml) olive oil, plus
  extra to brush and
  shallow-fry
2 tsp fish sauce
2 tbs plain flour
2 tsp each of ground
  coriander, cumin and
  paprika
½ tsp ground turmeric
4 x 180g swordfish or tuna
  steaks

Remove the skin and white pith from the lime. Holding the lime over a bowl to catch any juice, use a small sharp knife to cut the segments away from the inner membrane, then finely chop. Place chopped lime in a bowl with the avocado, cucumber, onion, chilli and coriander. Combine the oil, fish sauce and lime juice in a small bowl, then toss with the salsa. Set aside.

Combine the flour and dry spices in a shallow dish. Brush the fish with a little extra oil, then dip in the seasoned flour to coat, shaking off the excess.

Heat 2cm of olive oil in a large frypan over medium heat. Cook the fish, in batches if necessary, for 2–3 minutes each side until browned but still a little rare in the centre.

Serve the fish topped with the avocado salsa, with extra lime wedges to squeeze. **Serves 4**

Crumbed whiting with citrus salad

1 cup (150g) plain flour,
    seasoned with sea salt and
    freshly ground black
    pepper
2 eggs, lightly beaten
2 cups (100g) panko
    breadcrumbs*
600g skinless whiting fillets
1 tbs lemon juice
1 tbs white wine vinegar
1 tsp wholegrain mustard
1 tsp chopped lemon thyme
    or thyme leaves
½ cup (125ml) extra virgin
    olive oil
2 oranges, segmented
Small fennel bulb, thinly
    sliced
1 small frisee (curly endive)
1 cup (180g) nicoise or other
    small black olives
½ cup (150g) good-quality
    whole-egg mayonnaise
Sunflower oil, to deep-fry

Place flour, egg and breadcrumbs in 3 separate bowls. Dust fish first in flour, then dip in egg, then coat in crumbs. Transfer to a plate and refrigerate until needed.

To make dressing, combine lemon juice, vinegar, mustard and thyme in a bowl, then gradually whisk in olive oil. Season with sea salt and freshly ground black pepper. Set aside. Place orange, fennel, frisee and olives in a bowl and toss to combine. Set aside.

Place mayonnaise in a small bowl and loosen to a drizzling consistency with a little warm water. Set aside.

Half fill a deep-fryer or large saucepan with sunflower oil and heat to 190°C (a cube of bread will turn golden in 30 seconds when the oil is hot enough). Working in batches, gently lower fish into oil and deep-fry for 2–3 minutes until golden.

Add dressing to salad mixture and toss to combine. Serve immediately with fish and mayonnaise for drizzling. **Serves 4**

* Panko (extra-crispy Japanese breadcrumbs) are available from supermarkets; substitute dry breadcrumbs.

Spicy garlic prawns cooked in beer

1kg green king prawns, shells
   on, butterflied
80g unsalted butter
½ tsp smoked paprika
   (pimenton)
4 garlic cloves, finely
   chopped
Pinch of peri peri spice mix*
   or ½ tsp Tabasco (to taste)
¾ cup (185ml) lager
2 tbs chopped flat-leaf
   parsley
Shoestring fries, to serve

Melt 40g butter in a large frypan over medium-high heat. When sizzling, cook the prawns, in 2 batches, for 1 minute each side, then remove from the pan and set aside.

Melt the remaining 40g butter in the pan with the paprika, garlic and peri peri or Tabasco. Cook, stirring, for 1 minute until fragrant. Add the beer, increase the heat to high and cook for 2–3 minutes until the sauce thickens slightly. Remove from the heat, add the prawns and parsley and toss to combine.

Serve the prawns with shoestring fries and cold beer. **Serves 4**

* Peri peri spice mix is available from gourmet food shops and delis.

Salmon with tomato & coconut sambal

¼ cup (60ml) sunflower oil

2 Asian red eschalots*, thinly
   sliced

2 long green chillies, seeds
   removed, finely chopped

2cm piece ginger, grated

1 garlic clove, thinly sliced

2 tsp mild curry powder

10 fresh curry leaves*

250g cherry tomatoes, halved

270ml can coconut cream

Juice of 2 limes

4 salmon cutlets

Steamed rice, to serve

Coriander leaves, to garnish

Heat 2 tablespoons of the oil in a wok or saucepan over low heat. Add the eschalot, chilli, ginger and garlic and cook for 4–6 minutes until softened.

Add the curry powder, curry leaves and tomato, half the coconut cream and 2 tablespoons water and cook for 2–3 minutes until the tomato has started to break down slightly. Stir in the remaining coconut cream and lime juice, season to taste and simmer for 5 minutes until thickened slightly.

Meanwhile, heat the remaining oil in a frypan over medium-high heat. Season the salmon and cook for 2–3 minutes each side (or until cooked to your liking), then add to the sauce. Serve with rice, garnished with coriander. **Serves 4**

* Asian red eschalots are available from Asian food shops. Fresh curry leaves are available from selected greengrocers.

Fried squid with lime & ginger mayo

700g small squid
300ml soda water
2 cups (300g) plain flour
¼ tsp cayenne pepper
Sunflower or grapeseed oil*,
    to deep-fry
Lemon wedges, to serve

Lime & ginger mayonnaise
1 egg
1 tsp Dijon mustard
Finely grated zest and juice
    of 1 lime
300ml sunflower or grapeseed
    oil
2 tsp grated fresh ginger

For the mayonnaise, place the egg, mustard and half the lime juice in a bowl. Whisk to combine, then gradually add the oil drop by drop, whisking constantly until all the oil is incorporated and you have a thick mayonnaise. Stir in ginger and lime zest. Add remaining lime juice to taste, then season with salt and refrigerate until needed.

Separate the squid tubes from the tentacles. Clean the tubes, then slice into 1cm rings. Remove and discard the beaks from the tentacles. Place the rings and tentacles in a bowl, then pour over the soda water and leave for 20 minutes to tenderise.

Combine the flour, cayenne and 1 teaspoon sea salt in a bowl. Drain the squid, then toss in the flour mixture to coat.

Half fill a deep-fryer or large saucepan with oil and heat to 190°C. (A cube of bread will turn golden in 30 seconds when the oil is hot enough.) In batches, fry the squid for 1 minute or until just golden – any longer and it will become tough. Drain on paper towel, then sprinkle with salt and serve with the lime and ginger mayonnaise and lemon wedges. **Serves 4**

* Grapeseed oil is a light, flavourless oil, available from supermarkets.

Mexican chicken with smoky tomato salsa

¼ cup finely chopped
  flat-leaf parsley, plus
  2 cups whole flat-leaf
  parsley leaves
1 tbs ground cumin
½ cup (125ml) extra virgin
  olive oil
100ml lemon juice
4 chicken breast fillets with
  skin (wingbone attached
  – optional)*
2 vine-ripened tomatoes,
  seeds removed, thinly
  sliced
1 red onion, sliced into
  thin wedges
½ cup (40g) shaved parmesan

Smoky tomato salsa
3 red capsicums, quartered
5 vine-ripened tomatoes,
  halved, seeds removed
1 long red chilli, halved,
  seeds removed
1 garlic clove, chopped
1½ tbs red wine vinegar
¼ cup (60ml) extra
  virgin olive oil

Combine chopped parsley, cumin, half the oil and ¼ cup (60ml) lemon juice in a bowl. Season, then coat the chicken in the marinade. Cover and refrigerate for 30 minutes.

Meanwhile, for the smoky tomato salsa, place the capsicum, tomato and chilli, skin-side up, under a hot grill and cook for 5–6 minutes until the skins blacken. Place the capsicum and chilli in a plastic bag and seal, then set aside with the tomato to cool. When cool enough to handle, remove and discard the skin from the capsicum, chilli and tomato, then place the flesh in a food processor with the garlic, vinegar and oil. Season and blend until smooth. Transfer to a small saucepan and cook over medium heat for 10–12 minutes until thickened and reduced. Set aside.

Preheat a chargrill pan or barbecue to medium-high heat.

Cook the chicken for 3–4 minutes on each side until cooked through and golden brown. Keep warm.

Place the sliced tomato, red onion and whole parsley leaves in a bowl. Combine the remaining ¼ cup (60ml) oil and 2 tablespoons lemon juice in a bowl and season. Drizzle the dressing over the tomato and parsley salad and toss well to combine.

Spoon the tomato salsa onto serving plates with the salad. Place the chicken on top and garnish with parmesan, to serve. **Serves 4**

* Chicken breasts with wingbones attached are available from poultry shops and butchers.

Tunisian spiced chicken with hummus & pomegranate

1 tsp ground ginger

1 tsp mixed spice

½ tsp ground turmeric

2 tsp ground cumin

4 garlic cloves, finely
   chopped

½ cup (125ml) olive oil

Juice of 1 lemon, plus extra
   lemon wedges to serve

8 skinless chicken thigh fillets

1 small red onion, thinly
   sliced

2 cups picked watercress

Seeds of ½ pomegranate

½ tsp sumac*

4 warm flatbreads, quartered,
   to serve

350g tub good-quality
   hummus

Combine ginger, mixed spice, turmeric, cumin, garlic, ¼ cup (60ml) olive oil and half the lemon juice in a large bowl. Add chicken, turning to coat well. Cover and refrigerate for 1 hour.

Soak onion in a bowl of cold salted water for 15 minutes. Drain, then rinse and pat dry with paper towel. Combine onion, watercress and pomegranate seeds in a bowl, then set aside.

Heat a chargrill or frypan over medium-high heat. Drain chicken, then cook for 4–5 minutes each side until golden and cooked.

Toss salad with sumac, 2 tablespoons olive oil and remaining lemon juice. Season with sea salt and freshly ground black pepper.

Divide flatbreads among 4 plates and top with hummus, chicken and salad. Drizzle with remaining 1 tablespoon olive oil and serve with extra lemon wedges. **Serves 4**

* Sumac is a lemon-flavoured Middle Eastern spice made from ground dried berries, available from supermarkets and Middle Eastern food shops.

Quail under a brick with Asian gremolata

2 oranges

Finely grated zest and juice
of 1 lime

2 spring onions, finely
chopped

¼ cup (60ml) soy sauce

¼ cup (60ml) rice wine
vinegar

¼ cup (60ml) mirin

4 garlic cloves, finely
chopped

4 quails, butterflied*

¼ cup finely chopped
coriander leaves

¼ cup (35g) unsalted
peanuts, finely chopped

Sunflower oil, to brush

2 tbs crushed fried
Asian shallots*

Zest and juice 1 orange and combine with lime zest and juice in
a large ziplock bag. Add spring onion, soy sauce, vinegar, mirin and
three-quarters of the garlic. Add quails, seal bag and shake gently
to coat in marinade. Marinate in the fridge for 3–4 hours.

Meanwhile, for the Asian gremolata, zest remaining orange and
combine with remaining garlic, coriander and peanuts in a bowl.

Brush a chargrill or frypan with a little oil and heat over medium
heat. Place quails, skin-side down, on chargrill, then place a heavy
weight, such as foil-covered bricks or a heavy-based frypan, on
top and cook for 3 minutes. Remove weight, turn quails over and
replace weight, then cook for a further 2 minutes. Remove quails
from pan and rest, loosely covered with foil, for 4 minutes.

Combine fried Asian shallots with gremolata mixture and serve
sprinkled over quails. **Serves 4**

* Butterflied quails are available from selected supermarkets,
butchers and poultry shops. Fried Asian shallots are available
from Asian food shops and selected supermarkets.

Barbecue tapas

Large pinch of saffron threads

½ tsp coriander seeds

½ tsp cumin seeds

½ tsp fennel seeds

1 tsp sweet paprika

2 garlic cloves, chopped

¼ cup chopped
   oregano leaves

2 tsp red wine vinegar

1 tbs olive oil

2 x 170g skinless chicken
   breast fillets, cut into
   3cm pieces

4 chorizo sausages

400g can chopped tomatoes

2 tbs finely chopped
   flat-leaf parsley

Soak the saffron in 1 tablespoon boiling water for 10 minutes.

Meanwhile, place the coriander, cumin and fennel seeds in a dry frypan over low heat and cook, stirring, for 1 minute or until fragrant. Transfer to a mortar and pestle and pound until coarsely ground. Add the paprika, garlic, oregano, vinegar, saffron and soaking liquid and 2 teaspoons oil, then pound until a coarse paste. Transfer to a bowl and season, then add the chicken, tossing to coat well in the mixture. Cover and refrigerate for 2 hours to marinate.

Preheat the barbecue to medium heat.

Cut the chorizo on the diagonal into 2cm-thick slices and cook on the hotplate for 2 minutes each side until crispy and golden. Move the chorizo to one side of the hotplate to keep warm. Pour the tomato onto the hotplate, season well, and cook for 2–3 minutes until the juices have reduced and thickened. Toss with the chorizo and parsley. Keep warm.

Increase the heat to medium-high and brush the barbecue with remaining 2 teaspoons oil. Cook the chicken for 6–8 minutes, turning, until cooked through. Serve the chicken with the chorizo.
Serves 4

Wasabi crumbed chicken

2½ tbs wasabi paste

4 x 170g skinless chicken
   breast fillets

¼ cup (75g) whole-egg
   mayonnaise

75g wasabi peas*

1 cup (50g) panko
   breadcrumbs*

2 tbs cornflour

2 eggs, lightly beaten

Peanut oil, to shallow-fry, plus
   1 tbs extra

2 carrots, thinly sliced
   into matchsticks

2 celery stalks, thinly sliced
   into matchsticks

4 radishes, thinly sliced

150g snow peas, trimmed,
   thinly sliced into
   matchsticks

1 tbs soy sauce

1 tbs rice or white wine
   vinegar

Brush 2 teaspoons wasabi paste over each chicken breast and marinate in the fridge for 20 minutes. Combine the mayonnaise and remaining 2 teaspoons wasabi paste in a bowl and set aside.

Whiz wasabi peas in a food processor until roughly chopped, add breadcrumbs and pulse to combine. Transfer to a shallow bowl and season. Dust the chicken in the cornflour, shaking off excess, then dip in the egg and coat in crumb mixture.

Place a large frypan over medium-high heat and add 1cm oil. Shallow-fry chicken for 3 minutes each side or until crisp, golden and cooked through, then drain on paper towel.

Place the carrot, celery, radish and snow peas in a bowl. Whisk the soy sauce, vinegar and extra 1 tablespoon oil in a bowl, then season and toss with the salad to combine. Slice the chicken and serve with the salad and wasabi mayonnaise. **Serves 4**

* Wasabi peas and panko breadcrumbs (extra-crunchy Japanese breadcrumbs) are available from supermarkets; substitute dried breadcrumbs for the panko.

Panko-crumbed chicken Caesar salad

1 tbs grated ginger

1 tbs light soy sauce

2 tsp oyster sauce

2 tsp tomato sauce

2 tsp sesame oil

2 x 170g skinless chicken
breast fillets

1 baguette, thinly sliced

¼ cup (50g) rice flour

2 eggs, lightly beaten

2 cups (100g) panko
breadcrumbs*

Sunflower oil, to deep-fry

2 baby cos lettuce,
leaves separated

250g punnet cherry
tomatoes, halved

3 hard-boiled eggs, quartered

Shaved parmesan, to serve

Caesar salad dressing

1 egg

1 garlic clove, finely chopped

1 tsp Dijon mustard

½ tsp Worcestershire sauce

2 anchovy fillets in oil,
drained

150ml extra virgin olive oil

Juice of 1 lime

½ cup (40g) grated parmesan

Combine the ginger, soy sauce, oyster sauce, tomato sauce and sesame oil in a bowl. Cut the chicken into 2cm strips, then add to the soy mixture and toss to coat well. Cover and refrigerate for 2–3 hours.

Meanwhile, for the caesar salad dressing, place the egg, garlic, mustard, Worcestershire sauce and anchovies in a food processor and whiz to combine. With the motor running, slowly drizzle in the oil until thick and combined. Stir in the lime juice and parmesan, then season. Loosen with a little warm water if too thick. Keep chilled until ready to serve.

Heat a chargrill pan over medium-high heat. Lightly grill the baguette slices for 1–2 minutes each side until crispy. Set aside.

Drain the chicken from the marinade, allowing any excess to drip off. Place rice flour, egg and panko breadcrumbs in 3 separate bowls. Dip chicken first in the flour, then in the egg, then coat in the panko crumbs.

Half fill a deep-fryer or wok with oil and heat to 190°C. (A cube of bread will turn golden in 30 seconds.) In batches, fry the chicken for 2–3 minutes until crisp, golden and cooked through. Remove with a slotted spoon and drain on paper towel.

Place the lettuce, tomato, egg, baguette croutons and chicken in a large serving bowl and gently toss to combine. Top the salad with the shaved parmesan, drizzle with the dressing, then season well and serve. **Serves 4–6**

* Panko breadcrumbs (extra-crunchy Japanese breadcrumbs) are available from Asian food shops and supermarkets.

Oregano chicken on bean & olive salad

2 tbs dried oregano leaves

1 tsp dried red chilli flakes

Zest and juice of 1 lemon, plus lemon to serve

½ cup (125ml) extra virgin olive oil

4 corn-fed chicken breasts with skin* (wingbone attached, optional)

450g waxy potatoes (such as Anya or kipfler)

300g thin green beans, topped

1 small red onion, thinly sliced

2 tbs chopped flat-leaf parsley

100g pitted kalamata olives, crushed

2 tsp red wine vinegar

Mix the oregano, chilli, lemon zest and juice and ⅓ cup (80ml) of the oil in a bowl with salt and pepper. Make a few slashes in the chicken skin, then place chicken in a shallow dish and rub in the marinade, making sure it's well coated. Cover and marinate in the fridge for 1–2 hours.

Meanwhile, make the salad. Boil the potatoes in a pan of salted water for 8–10 minutes until just tender. Drain, return to the pan and lightly crush. Blanch the beans in boiling salted water for 2 minutes, then drain. Place in a large bowl with the crushed potatoes, remaining oil, onion, parsley, olives and vinegar. Season well, then set aside while you cook the chicken.

Meanwhile, preheat a chargrill pan or barbecue on medium-high. Grill the chicken for 5–6 minutes each side until cooked through (if browning too quickly, finish cooking in the oven).

Serve the chicken on the salad, with extra lemon to squeeze.

Serves 4

* Corn fed chicken breasts are available from poultry shops and butchers.

Quail with rose petals and yoghurt

4 garlic cloves,
    finely chopped
2 tsp mixed spice
2 tsp ground cumin
⅓ cup (80ml) rosewater
⅓ cup (80ml) lemon juice
¼ cup (60ml) extra
    virgin olive oil
8 quails*, butterflied
½ cup (160g) rose-petal
    jelly* or quince paste,
    plus extra to serve
Thick Greek-style yoghurt,
    dried edible rose petals*
    and rocket leaves, to serve

Place the garlic and half of each of the spices, rosewater, lemon juice and oil in a dish. Coat the quail in the marinade, then cover and refrigerate for at least 4 hours or overnight.

Place the remaining spices, rosewater, lemon juice and oil in a saucepan over low heat with the rose-petal jelly and warm gently, stirring until the jelly is melted and smooth. Set aside.

Preheat a chargrill pan or barbecue to medium-high heat.

Season the quail and cook for 3–4 minutes each side until charred and cooked through. Divide quail among serving plates, drizzle with the rose-petal sauce and yoghurt and scatter with rose petals and rocket leaves. Serve with extra rose-petal jelly. **Serves 4**

* Quail is available from selected butchers; ask your butcher to butterfly the quail. Rose-petal jelly and dried rose petals are available from Middle Eastern food shops and gourmet food shops.

Spicy chicken with spoon salad

4 chicken breast fillets

4 tsp harissa*

⅓ cup (80ml) olive oil

5 vine-ripened tomatoes

1 roasted red capsicum*,
   chopped

2 small red chillies, seeds
   removed, finely chopped

2 eschalots or ½ red onion,
   finely chopped

½ telegraph cucumber,
   peeled, seeds removed,
   finely chopped

2 tbs finely chopped flat-leaf
   parsley

1 tbs finely chopped mint

1 tbs sherry vinegar*
   or red wine vinegar

Couscous, to serve

Greek-style yoghurt and pita,
   to serve (optional)

Make 3 shallow slashes in each chicken breast. Combine 2 teaspoons harissa and 2 tablespoons olive oil in a bowl, then brush all over the chicken. Cover and marinate in the fridge while you make the salad.

For the spoon salad, bring a pan of water to the boil. Cut a cross in the base of each tomato, then place in boiling water for 30 seconds. Plunge into a bowl of iced water. Once cool enough to handle, peel the tomatoes, then halve, remove seeds and finely chop. Place the chopped tomato in a bowl with the capsicum, chilli, eschalot, cucumber, parsley, mint, vinegar and remaining harissa and olive oil. Season well with salt and pepper and toss to combine, then place in a sieve set over the bowl and allow to drain for 30 minutes to remove excess liquid.

Preheat a chargrill pan or barbecue to medium-high heat. Cook the chicken for 6–7 minutes each side, turning occasionally, until cooked through. Slice the chicken, then top with the spoon salad and serve with couscous, yoghurt and pita, if desired. **Serves 4**

* Harissa (a Tunisian chilli paste), roasted capsicum and sherry vinegar are available from gourmet food shops and delis.

Pork cutlets with peach pan chutney

4 garlic cloves, finely
   chopped
2cm piece ginger, grated
1 tsp mild curry powder
100ml olive oil
4 French-trimmed pork
   cutlets
2 large yellow peaches
4 vine-ripened tomatoes
1 onion, finely chopped
2 tsp caster sugar
2 tbs red wine vinegar
Coriander sprigs and green
   salad (optional), to serve

Combine the garlic, ginger, curry powder and ¼ cup (60ml) oil in a glass or ceramic dish. Season with salt and pepper, then add the pork cutlets and turn to coat in the mixture. Cover and marinate in the fridge for at least 10 minutes, or up to 2 hours.

Meanwhile, cut a cross in the base of the peaches and tomatoes. Blanch in boiling water for 1 minute, then plunge into a bowl of iced water. When cool enough to handle, peel, remove and discard tomato seeds and peach stones. Chop the flesh and set aside.

Preheat the oven to 180°C.

Heat 1 tablespoon oil in a large frypan over medium-high heat. Add the pork cutlets and cook for 2 minutes each side or until lightly browned. Place on a baking tray and cook in the oven for 10 minutes or until cooked through.

Meanwhile, return the pan to medium-low heat and add 1 tablespoon oil. Add the onion and cook, stirring occasionally, for 2–3 minutes until softened. Add the peach and tomato and cook, stirring, for 4–5 minutes until they soften and start to break down. Stir in the sugar and vinegar, then simmer for 3–4 minutes until thickened and lightly caramelised. Serve the pork with the pan chutney, coriander and a green salad, if desired. **Serves 4**

Sausage saltimbocca

8 thin prosciutto slices
16 sage leaves
8 good-quality pork
    chipolatas or other thin
    pork sausages
2 tbs plain flour, seasoned
¼ cup (60ml) olive oil
30g unsalted butter
150ml dry white wine
8 dinner rolls
1 garlic clove, halved
Rocket leaves, to serve

Lay the prosciutto slices on a clean chopping board. Place 1 fresh sage leaf at the end of each slice. Place a sausage at the other end, then roll up to enclose the sausage in the prosciutto (making sure the sage leaf is visible). Secure with a cocktail stick or toothpick. Repeat with the remaining sausages. Toss the sausages in the seasoned flour, shaking off any excess.

Heat the oil in a large frypan over medium-high heat. Add the remaining sage leaves and cook for 1 minute or until crisp, then remove and drain on paper towel.

Drain all but 1 tablespoon oil from the pan, then add 2 teaspoons butter and place over medium heat. Cook the sausages, turning, for 4–5 minutes until cooked through. Transfer to a plate and keep warm.

Add the wine to the pan and allow to bubble for 3–4 minutes until the sauce thickens slightly. Add the remaining 20g butter and swirl to form a sauce, then season.

Meanwhile, split the rolls in half and place under a hot grill until lightly toasted. Rub the bread with the cut-side of the garlic clove. Place rolls on serving plates, top with sausages and rocket, drizzle with the sauce and garnish with fried sage. **Serves 4**

Spanish eggs

500g pontiac or desiree
  potatoes, peeled, cut into
  2cm cubes
2½ tbs olive oil
1 red onion, thinly sliced
2 garlic cloves, finely
  chopped
1 chorizo sausage, cut into
  2cm pieces
1½ tsp smoked paprika
  (pimenton)
½ tsp ground cumin
280g jar chargrilled or
  roasted red capsicum*,
  drained, chopped
4 free-range eggs
1 tbs finely chopped flat-leaf
  parsley

Cook the potato in a pan of boiling salted water for 2–3 minutes until just tender, then drain and set aside.

Heat 2 tablespoons oil in a large frypan over medium heat. Add the onion and cook, stirring, for 2–3 minutes until just soft. Add the garlic, chorizo, potato, paprika and cumin and cook, stirring, for a further 2–3 minutes until the chorizo and potato start to crisp. Add the chargrilled capsicum, season well, then cook over low heat until heated through.

Meanwhile, brush a non-stick frypan with the remaining oil and place over medium heat. Break the eggs, one at a time, into the pan. Cover with a lid and cook for 2 minutes until the eggwhites are cooked but the yolks are still soft.

Divide the potato mixture among warm plates, top with an egg, sprinkle with parsley, season with salt and pepper, then serve.
Serves 4

* Chargrilled capsicum is available from supermarkets.

Spanish pork with orange & poppyseed salad

1 tsp cumin

1 tbs smoked paprika (pimenton)

Zest and juice of 1 orange

⅓ cup (80ml) tomato sauce (ketchup)

⅓ cup (80ml) maple syrup

2 pork fillets (about 500g each), trimmed, halved

Orange & poppyseed salad

2 oranges

3 Lebanese cucumbers, halved lengthways, seeds removed, sliced

¼ cup coriander leaves

2 long red chillies, seeds removed, finely chopped

⅓ cup (80ml) white wine vinegar

½ cup (125ml) olive oil

2 tbs caster sugar

2 tbs poppyseeds

Place cumin, paprika, orange zest and juice, tomato sauce and maple syrup in a zip-lock bag with the pork and shake well to coat pork. Marinate in the fridge for at least 1 hour or overnight.

For the salad, zest the rind of 1 orange and set aside in a small bowl. Peel both oranges, then halve and slice the flesh. Place in a large bowl with the cucumber, coriander and chilli. Add the vinegar, oil, sugar and poppyseeds to the zest bowl, season well and whisk to combine. Set salad and dressing aside.

Preheat a chargrill pan or barbecue on medium-high heat.

Cook the pork, turning, for 5–6 minutes until blackened on the outside and cooked through. Set aside loosely covered with foil for 5 minutes to rest, then slice. Divide the salad mixture among 4 plates, top with the sliced pork, then drizzle with dressing.

Serves 4

Pea pancakes with crisp pancetta and sweet chilli sauce

1 cup (160g) fresh, podded
   or (120g) frozen peas
3 eggs
1 cup (240g) fresh ricotta,
   drained
¼ cup (35g) plain flour
1 tbs olive oil, plus extra
   to fry
4 spring onions, finely
   chopped
8 slices round pancetta
   or streaky bacon
Shop-bought sweet chilli
   sauce, sour cream and
   pea tendrils or watercress
   sprigs, to serve

Cook fresh peas in a saucepan of boiling salted water for 5 minutes or frozen peas for 2 minutes. Drain, refresh in iced water, then drain well.

Place eggs, ricotta, flour and oil in a food processor. Season with sea salt and freshly ground black pepper, then process until smooth. Transfer to a bowl and stir in peas and spring onion (add a little cold water if the batter is too thick; it should be the consistency of pancake batter). Set aside for 30 minutes.

Meanwhile, preheat the grill to high.

Place pancetta on a baking tray and grill until crisp and golden. Drain on paper towel and keep warm.

Heat a little oil in a non-stick frypan over medium-high heat. Add generous tablespoon of batter to the frypan, in batches, and cook for 1–2 minutes until golden underneath, then flip and cook for a further 1–2 minutes. Keep warm and repeat with remaining batter.

Layer pancakes and pancetta on a serving plate and serve with sweet chilli sauce, sour cream and pea tendrils. **Serves 4**

Vineyard sausages

1 tbs extra virgin olive oil,
   plus extra to drizzle
12 pork chipolatas (or use
   4 chicken or pork sausages)
1 eschalot, finely chopped
2 cups (350g) mixed seedless
   grapes
½ cup (125ml) dry white wine
2 tsp chopped rosemary
   leaves
2 tsp honey
Grilled bread and chopped
   chives, to serve

Heat the olive oil in a frypan over medium-high heat. Add the
sausages and cook, turning, for 8–10 minutes until cooked through
and golden. Remove the sausages to a plate, cover with foil and
keep warm.

Drain any excess fat from the frypan, then return the pan to
medium heat. Add the eschalot and grapes and cook, stirring, for
3–4 minutes until the grapes start to soften and begin to lose their
juice. Add the wine, rosemary and honey, then stir for a further
minute until heated through. Serve the sausages and grape mixture
over grilled bread, drizzled with extra oil and sprinkled with chives.
Serves 4

Sausages with red cabbage and onion jam

1 cup (150g) currants

30g unsalted butter

1 tbs olive oil

4 (about 400g) red onions,
  thinly sliced

½ small red cabbage,
  very thinly sliced

1 garlic clove, chopped

½ tsp ground cinnamon

½ tsp freshly grated nutmeg

⅓ cup (75g) brown sugar

½ cup (125ml) good-quality
  balsamic vinegar

8 good-quality pork
  or beef sausages

Soak the currants in boiling water for 15 minutes, then drain.

Melt the butter with the oil in a large saucepan over medium-low heat. Add the onion and 1 teaspoon salt and cook, stirring, for 20–25 minutes until soft and lightly caramelised. Add the cabbage, garlic and spices and cook, stirring occasionally for 20–25 minutes until very tender. Add the sugar, balsamic vinegar and drained currants and cook for a further 10 minutes or until thick and syrupy.

Meanwhile, preheat a chargrill pan or barbecue to medium heat.

Cook the sausages, turning, until evenly browned and cooked through. Serve with the red cabbage and onion jam. **Serves 4**

Fried eggs with bacon jam

500g smoked bacon, rind
   removed, finely chopped
1 onion, finely chopped
4 garlic cloves, finely
   chopped
½ cup firmly packed (125g)
   dark brown sugar
¼ cup (60ml) bourbon
½ cup (125ml) freshly brewed
   espresso
2 tbs sherry or balsamic
   vinegar
¼ cup (60ml) maple syrup
4 eggs

Cook bacon in a frypan over medium heat, stirring occasionally, for 3–4 minutes, until most of the fat has rendered. Remove bacon with a slotted spoon and drain on paper towel. Pour off the melted fat and reserve, leaving 1 tablespoon fat in the pan.

Reduce heat to medium-low, then add the onion and cook, stirring occasionally, for 5–6 minutes until golden. Add garlic and stir to combine, then add sugar, bourbon, espresso, vinegar, maple syrup, cooked bacon and ½ cup (125ml) water. Season with sea salt and freshly ground black pepper, then increase heat to medium-high and bring to a simmer. Reduce heat to low and cook, stirring occasionally, for 1 hour or until the mixture is a jammy consistency. Makes 2 cups.

Heat a little of the reserved bacon fat in a frypan and fry eggs to your liking. Serve with spoonfuls of bacon jam. **Serves 4**

XO pork stir-fry with Asian greens

3 tbs XO sauce*

½ tsp sesame oil

1½ tsp chilli jam*

1 tbs honey

1 tbs light soy sauce

1 tbs sunflower oil

300g pork fillet, thinly sliced

1 garlic clove, thinly sliced

3cm piece ginger, thinly
   sliced

3 spring onions, thinly sliced

1 tbs Chinese rice wine
   (shaohsing)*

1 bunch Chinese broccoli
   (gai lan) or other Asian
   greens

Steamed rice, to serve

Combine the XO sauce, sesame oil, chilli jam, honey and soy sauce in a bowl.

Heat the sunflower oil in a wok over high heat. When the oil is smoking, add half the pork and stir-fry for 1–2 minutes until browned. Remove and repeat with the remaining pork.

Decrease the heat to medium and return all the browned pork to the wok. Add the garlic, ginger and half the onion and stir-fry for 1 minute until fragrant. Add the wine and XO mixture and stir-fry for a further minute.

Meanwhile, steam the Chinese broccoli over a pan of boiling water for 2–3 minutes until just tender and bright green. Serve with the pork stir-fry on steamed rice. **Serves 4**

* XO sauce and Chinese rice wine are available from Asian food shops. Chilli jam is available from supermarkets and delis.

Grilled zucchini wraps

2 tbs olive oil

2 garlic cloves,
   finely chopped

2 long zucchini, trimmed,
   quartered lengthways

1 cup (160g) podded fresh
   or frozen (120g) peas

80g marinated feta, drained

¼ cup (70g) thick Greek-style
   yoghurt

2 spring onions, finely
   chopped, plus extra, thinly
   sliced on an angle to serve

Finely grated zest and juice
   of 1 lemon

4 butter lettuce leaves

4 flour tortillas, lightly
   chargrilled

½ cup mint leaves

1 long red chilli, seeds
   removed, finely shredded

Combine olive oil and garlic in a bowl. Brush zucchini all over with garlic oil and season with sea salt and freshly ground black pepper.

Preheat a chargrill over high heat. Add zucchini, flesh-side down, then cover loosely with foil and cook for 3 minutes or until lightly charred. Turn and cook the other flesh side for a further 3 minutes or until lightly charred (don't cook the skin side, as it will burn).

Meanwhile, cook peas in a saucepan of boiling salted water for 3 minutes for fresh and 2 minutes for frozen. Drain, set aside one-third of the peas, then roughly crush the remainder with a fork.

Combine crushed peas with the drained feta and yoghurt in a bowl. Add spring onion, lemon zest and lemon juice, to taste, then season well.

To serve, place a lettuce leaf on each tortilla, top with pea mixture, then place 2 wedges of zucchini on top. Scatter with reserved peas, mint leaves, chilli and extra spring onion, then roll up tightly to eat. **Serves 4 as a side**

Haloumi with Mediterranean salad

200g fregola*

6 roma tomatoes (about
   360g), seeds removed,
   chopped

12 pitted kalamata olives,
   chopped

12 pitted green olives,
   chopped

6 marinated artichokes,
   drained, chopped

1 spring onion, finely
   chopped

1 tbs baby capers, rinsed,
   drained

1 preserved lemon quarter*,
   white pith removed, rind
   finely chopped

30g toasted pine nuts

¼ cup mint leaves, plus
   extra leaves to garnish

1 tbs chopped flat-leaf
   parsley

1 tbs chopped basil

250g haloumi cheese, cut into
   wedges

¼ cup (60ml) extra virgin
   olive oil, plus extra to brush

2 tbs lemon juice, plus
   lemon wedges to serve

Cook the fregola according to packet instructions, then place
in a bowl and toss with the tomato, olives, artichokes, spring onion,
capers, preserved lemon rind, pine nuts and herbs. Set aside.

Preheat a chargrill pan or barbecue to medium-high heat.

Rinse the haloumi under cold water to remove any excess salt,
then pat dry with paper towel and brush with olive oil. Grill for
1 minute each side until crispy and golden. Keep warm.

Whisk the oil and lemon juice together, season, then drizzle over
the salad and toss to combine. Top the salad with the haloumi,
garnish with extra mint leaves and serve with lemon wedges.

Serves 4

* Fregola (small Sardinian pasta) and preserved lemon
are available from delis.

Beet burgers

30g unsalted butter

1 large (200g) raw beetroot,
   coarsely grated

1 onion, grated

1 tbs red wine vinegar

300g mashed potato

1 tbs sour cream,
   plus extra to serve

1 tsp bottled horseradish,
   plus extra to serve

Sunflower oil, to shallow-fry

Plain flour, to dust

4 burger buns, toasted

Sliced tomatoes, snow pea
   sprouts, sliced avocado,
   sliced red onion and salad
   leaves, to serve

Melt butter in a frypan over low heat, add beetroot, onion and vinegar, and cook, stirring, for 10 minutes or until softened. Combine in a bowl with mashed potato, sour cream and horseradish, then season with sea salt and freshly ground black pepper. Form into 4 round patties, then refrigerate for 20 minutes to firm up.

Heat 1cm oil in a frypan over medium-high heat. Dust beetroot patties all over with a little flour, then cook for 2 minutes each side or until golden. Serve in a toasted burger bun with tomato, snow pea sprouts, avocado, red onion and salad leaves, topped with extra sour cream and horseradish. **Makes 4**

Asparagus bruschetta with poached eggs and pecorino

2 bunches asparagus,
   ends trimmed
2 cups (300g) fresh podded
   or frozen broad beans
60g unsalted butter
1 tbs lemon juice
1 tsp white wine vinegar
4 eggs
4 slices sourdough
Olive oil, to brush and drizzle
1 garlic clove, halved
30g shaved pecorino cheese*

Blanch the asparagus and broad beans in boiling salted water for 2 minutes or until just tender. Drain and refresh in cold water, then remove the outer skins from the broad beans. Melt the butter in a frypan over medium heat. Add the asparagus and broad beans and cook for 1 minute, tossing to coat in the butter. Add the lemon juice and toss to combine, then remove from the heat and set aside.

Meanwhile, bring a shallow pan of water to the boil, add white vinegar, then reduce heat to medium-low. Break eggs into the simmering water and poach for 5 minutes until white is cooked through but yolk is still soft. Remove with a slotted spoon. Keep warm.

Chargrill the bread for 1–2 minutes each side until lightly charred. Rub the toast with the cut side of the garlic and brush with oil. Arrange the vegetables on the toast, sit a poached egg on top, then scatter with cheese and drizzle with oil. Season with sea salt and freshly ground black pepper, then serve. **Serves 4**

* Pecorino is a hard sheep's milk cheese, available from delis; substitute parmesan.

Eggplant pesto timballos

2 garlic cloves, finely
  chopped
½ cup (125ml) extra virgin
  olive oil
2 (about 600g) eggplants,
  cut into 1cm-thick slices
1¼ cups (300g) ricotta
200g jar good-quality pesto
250g punnet vine-ripened
  cherry tomatoes
¼ cup basil leaves

Heat a chargrill pan or barbecue to medium-high heat.

Combine garlic and ⅓ cup (80ml) oil in a bowl. Brush both sides of the eggplant slices with the garlic oil. In batches if necessary, cook the eggplant for 1 minute on one side, then turn at a 90° angle and cook for a further 1 minute – this will create a crisscross pattern on the eggplant slices. Turn the eggplant and repeat the process on the other side. Set aside to cool.

Preheat the oven to 200°C. Grease 4 x 1-cup (250ml) ramekins.

Place ricotta in a bowl and season. Place 1 chargrilled eggplant slice in each ramekin and top with 1 heaped tablespoon seasoned ricotta, then a tablespoonful of pesto. Repeat the layers with the remaining eggplant, ricotta and pesto, finishing each timballo with an eggplant slice.

Place the ramekins on a baking tray and bake for 15 minutes. Remove the baking tray from the oven and place the tomatoes on the tray with the timballos. Drizzle the tomatoes with 1 tablespoon olive oil, season, then return the tray to the oven for a further 8 minutes or until the tomatoes have just started to soften and the timballos are warmed through. Remove from the oven and rest for 5 minutes.

Heat remaining tablespoon of oil in a small frypan over medium heat and carefully cook the basil leaves for 15 seconds or until crispy. Remove the basil from the pan with a slotted spoon and drain on paper towel.

Invert the timballos onto serving plates and season. Garnish with the roasted tomatoes and fried basil leaves and serve. **Serves 4**

Asparagus with crumbed haloumi

1 tbs honey

1 tsp Dijon mustard

2 tbs cider vinegar

⅓ cup (80ml) extra virgin olive oil

300g asparagus, trimmed, chargrilled or blanched

3 oranges, peeled, segmented

1 cup wild rocket

½ cup (75g) plain flour, seasoned with sea salt and freshly ground black pepper

2 eggs, lightly beaten

1 cup (50g) panko breadcrumbs*

¼ cup (20g) grated parmesan

300g haloumi, drained, thickly sliced into triangles

Olive oil, to shallow-fry

Sprigs of fresh herbs (such as tarragon) to garnish

Whisk together honey, mustard, vinegar and extra virgin olive oil in a bowl.

Combine asparagus, orange and rocket in a bowl.

Place flour and egg in separate bowls. Combine breadcrumbs and parmesan in a third bowl. Dust haloumi first in flour, shaking off excess, then dip in egg, then breadcrumb mixture. Refrigerate for 15 minutes to firm up.

Heat 1cm olive oil in a large frypan over medium-high heat and fry haloumi, in batches if necessary, for 1 minute each side or until crisp and golden.

To serve, add dressing to salad, toss to combine and top with crumbed haloumi and fresh herbs. **Serves 4**

* Panko breadcrumbs (extra-crunchy Japanese breadcrumbs) are available from supermarkets; substitute dry breadcrumbs.

Spinach gnudi with sage burnt butter

150g English spinach,
  stems removed
1½ cups (360g) fresh ricotta,
  well drained
Pinch of ground nutmeg
¾ cup (60g) finely grated
  parmesan, plus extra
  to serve
2 egg yolks, lightly beaten
½ cup (75g) plain flour, sifted,
  plus extra to dust
100g unsalted butter
16 sage leaves

Cook the spinach leaves in saucepan of boiling, salted water for 1 minute or until just wilted. Drain and refresh under cold water, then squeeze out as much liquid as possible.

Finely chop the spinach, then place in a bowl with the ricotta, nutmeg, parmesan and egg. Season and stir to combine, then mix in the flour. The mixture should be slightly sticky, but not too wet – add a little more flour if needed. Shape the ricotta mixture into walnut-sized balls, then lightly dust with flour.

In batches, cook the gnudi in a large saucepan of salted, simmering water for 1–2 minutes until they rise to the surface. Remove with a slotted spoon and set aside on a plate.

Meanwhile, melt the butter in a frypan over medium heat. Add the sage and cook for 2–3 minutes until the sage is crisp and the butter is just starting to brown.

Add the gnudi to the frypan and gently toss to combine. Divide gnudi and sage burnt butter among plates and serve sprinkled with extra parmesan. **Serves 4**

Crispy polenta with truffled mushrooms & Taleggio

2 cups (500ml) chicken or
  vegetable stock
½ cup (85g) instant polenta
1 cup (80g) finely grated
  parmesan
30g unsalted butter, chopped
½ cup (125ml) olive oil
350g mixed mushrooms
  (such as chestnut and king
  brown), sliced if large
2 garlic cloves, finely
  chopped
1 tbs chopped thyme leaves
1 tbs chopped tarragon
  leaves
1 tbs truffle oil*, plus extra
  to serve
100g Taleggio or other soft
  washed-rind cheese, rind
  removed, chopped
Chopped flat-leaf parsley
  leaves, to serve

Place the stock in a saucepan over medium-high heat. Bring to the boil, then reduce heat to low. Pour in the polenta in a slow, steady stream and cook, stirring constantly, for 2–3 minutes until thick. Stir in the parmesan and butter, season, then pour into a lightly oiled 16cm x 10cm plastic container or baking pan. Cool, then chill for 30 minutes or until firm. Cut the polenta into 8 x 8cm long rectangles.

Heat ⅓ cup (80ml) olive oil in a frypan over medium-high heat. In batches, fry the polenta for 2–3 minutes each side until a golden crust forms. Keep warm.

Wipe the frypan clean with paper towel, then add the remaining 2 tablespoons olive oil and place over high heat. In 2 batches, pan-fry the mushrooms for 2–3 minutes until just starting to soften. Return all the mushrooms to the pan with the garlic, thyme, tarragon and truffle oil, season, then cook, stirring, for a further 1 minute.

Divide the polenta among plates, top with the mushroom mixture and dot with the Taleggio, allowing it to melt slightly. Sprinkle with parsley, drizzle with extra truffle oil and serve. **Serves 4**

* Truffle oil is available from delis and gourmet food shops; substitute extra virgin olive oil.

Strawberry & brie sandwiches

40g unsalted butter

8 slices brioche

50g strawberry jam

250g strawberries, hulled,
  sliced

175g chilled brie, sliced
  1cm-thick

1–2 tbs caster sugar

Icing sugar, to dust

Use half the butter to spread on the brioche slices. Spread the unbuttered sides of 4 slices with jam, then cover with the strawberry slices and brie. Top with the remaining brioche, unbuttered-side down, then sprinkle the sandwiches all over with the caster sugar.

Melt the remaining butter in a frypan over medium heat. Add two sandwiches and cook for 1–2 minutes each side, pressing down gently with a spatula, until the bread is golden and the brie has melted. Keep warm while you cook the remaining sandwiches, then serve dusted with icing sugar. **Makes 4**

Index

asparagus
  bruschetta with poached eggs
    and pecorino 114
  with crumbed haloumi 118

barbecue tapas 78
barbecued prawn cocktails 44
bean and olive salad with oregano
    chicken 84
beef
  bulgogi with easy pickled
    vegetables 12
  eye fillet with raspberry sauce 24
  green tea yakitori with Japanese
    seasoned rice 26
  lemongrass skewers with cucumber
    salad 6
  Moorish skewers with cauliflower
    couscous 14
  sausages with red cabbage and
    onion jam 102
  see also steak
beet burgers 112
black vinegar dressing 54
brie and strawberry sandwiches 124
broad bean salad with lamb and
    preserved lemon meatballs 36
bruschetta with asparagus, poached
    eggs and pecorino 114
bulgogi with easy pickle 12
burgers
  beet 112
  pepper steak 18
  tuna wasabi 50
  vitello tonnato (veal) 8

Caesar salad
  dressing 82
  with panko-crumbed chicken 82
calamari with Greek salad 52
cauliflower couscous with Moorish
    beef skewers 14
cevapi 20
chermoula fish with tahini sauce 60
chicken
  and chorizo tapas 78
  Caesar salad 82
  Mexican, with smoky tomato
    salsa 72

oregano, on bean and olive salad 84
  spicy, with spoon salad 88
  Tunisian spiced, with hummus and
    pomegranate 74
  wasabi crumbed 80
chickpea and bean salad with
    zaatar-crusted lamb 38
chorizo and chicken tapas 78
cocktail sauce 44
corn cakes (Mexican) with avocado
    and prawns 58
crumbed whiting with citrus salad 64
cucumber salad with beef on
    lemongrass skewers 6
curried sausages 22
curry dressing 56
cutlets (lamb)
  herb-rubbed, with pea and feta
    salad 34
  with spiced vegetable chips 28
cutlets (pork) with peach pan
    chutney 90

dressings
  black vinegar 54
  Caesar salad 82
  curry 56
  lime and ginger mayo 70
  lime 42
  tahini 38
  vinaigrette 52
dumplings: spinach gnudi with sage
    burnt butter 120

eggplant pesto timballos 116
eggs
  fried, with bacon jam 104
  poached, on bruschetta with
    asparagus and pecorino 114
  Spanish 94
eye fillet with raspberry sauce 24

fennel and orange salad with salmon
    skewers 42
fish
  chermoula fish with tahini sauce 60
  crumbed whiting with citrus salad 64
  pan-fried, with malt vinegar
    tartare 46
  salmon skewers with fennel and
    orange salad 42
  salmon with tomato and coconut
    sambal 68

spicy swordfish with avocado and
    lime salsa 62
  tea 'smoked' salmon 48
  tuna with green tea noodles and
    black vinegar dressing 54
  tuna wasabi burgers 50
fried eggs with bacon jam 104
fried squid with lime and ginger
    mayo 70

garlic prawns (spicy) cooked in beer 66
gnudi (spinach) with sage burnt
    butter 120
Greek salad with calamari 52
green tea yakitori with Japanese
    seasoned rice 26
grilled zucchini wraps 108

haloumi
  crumbed, with asparagus 118
  with Mediterranean salad 110
herb-rubbed lamb cutlets with
    pea and feta salad 34
hummus, hot and fiery 40

kebabs
  rosemary lamb, with lemon and
    olive relish 30
  see also skewers

lamb
  cutlets with pea and feta salad 34
  cutlets with spiced vegetable
    chips 28
  kebabs with lemon and olive
    relish 30
  and preserved lemon meatballs with
    crushed broad bean salad 36
  wraps 32
  zaatar-crusted, with chickpea and
    bean salad 38
lime and ginger mayo 70

mayo: lime and ginger 70
meatballs of lamb and preserved
    lemon, with crushed broad bean
    salad 36
Mediterranean salad with haloumi 110
Mexican chicken with smoky tomato
    salsa 72
Mexican corn cakes with avocado
    and prawns 58
Mexican steak sandwich 16

Moorish beef skewers with
cauliflower couscous 14
mushrooms (truffled) with Taleggio
and crispy polenta 122

orange and poppyseed salad 96
oregano chicken on bean and olive
salad 84

pancakes (pea) with crisp pancetta
and sweet chilli sauce 98
pan-fried fish with malt vinegar
tartare 46
panko-crumbed chicken Caesar
salad 82
pea
and feta salad with herb-rubbed
lamb cutlets 34
pancakes with crisp pancetta and
sweet chilli sauce 98
pepper steak burger 18
pickled vegetables
carrot and daikon 12
cucumber and carrots 50
poached eggs, asparagus and
pecorino bruschetta 114
polenta with truffled mushrooms
and Taleggio 122
pork
cutlets with peach pan chutney 90
sausage saltimbocca 92
sausages with red cabbage and
onion jam 102
Spanish, with orange and
poppyseed salad 96
vineyard sausages 100
XO stir-fry with Asian greens 106
prawns
and avocado with Mexican corn
cakes 58
cocktails 44
spicy garlic, cooked in beer 66

quail
with Asian gremolata 76
with rose petals and yoghurt 86

rosemary lamb kebabs with lemon
and olive relish 30

salad
bean and olive, with oregano
chicken 84

broad bean, with lamb and
preserved lemon meatballs 36
Caesar, with panko-crumbed
chicken 82
chickpea and bean, with zaatar-
crusted lamb 38
citrus, with crumbed whiting 64
cucumber, with beef on lemongrass
skewers 6
fennel and orange, with salmon
skewers 42
Greek, with calamari 52
Mediterranean, with haloumi 110
orange and poppyseed, 96
pea and feta, with herb-rubbed
lamb cutlets 34
spoon, with spicy chicken 88
salmon
skewers with fennel and orange
salad 42
tea 'smoked' 48
with tomato and coconut
sambal 68
salsa, tomato 72
saltimbocca, sausage 92
sauces
cocktail 44
lime and ginger mayo 70
tonnato 8
see also dressings
sausages
cevapi 20
curried 22
with red cabbage and onion
jam 102
saltimbocca 92
vineyard 100
scallops with cauliflower skordalia
and curry dressing 56
seafood see calamari; fish; prawns;
scallops; squid
skewers
beef on lemongrass with cucumber
salad 6
Moorish beef with cauliflower
couscous 14
rosemary lamb with lemon and
olive relish 30
salmon with fennel and orange
salad 42
Spanish eggs 94
Spanish pork with orange and
poppyseed salad 96

spinach gnudi with sage burnt
butter 120
spoon salad with spicy chicken 88
squid (fried), with lime and ginger
mayo 70
steak
burger, pepper 18
sandwich, Mexican 16
with simple bearnaise 10
strawberry and brie sandwiches 124
swordfish (spicy), with avocado and
lime salsa 62

tahini dressing 38
tapas, barbecue 78
tea 'smoked' salmon 48
timballos: eggplant pesto 116
tomato salsa 72
tonnato sauce 8
tuna
with green tea noodles and black
vinegar dressing 54
wasabi burgers 50
Tunisian spiced chicken with hummus
and pomegranate 74

veal burgers 8
vegetable chips with lamb cutlets 28
vinaigrette 52
vineyard sausages 100
vitello tonnato burgers 8

wasabi crumbed chicken 80
whiting (crumbed), with citrus salad 64
wraps
grilled zucchini 108
lamb 32

XO pork stir-fry with Asian greens 106

yakitori with Japanese seasoned
rice 26
zaatar-crusted lamb with chickpea
and bean salad 38

zucchini wraps 108

The ABC 'Wave' device is a trademark of the
Australian Broadcasting Corporation and is used
under licence by HarperCollinsPublishers Australia.

delicious. Sizzle comprises recipes and photographs originally published in delicious. Faking It (2008),
delicious. Quick Smart Cook (2009), delicious. More Please (2010), delicious. Simply the Best (2011),
delicious. Home Cooking (2012) and delicious. Love to Cook (2013)

First published in Australia in 2015
by HarperCollinsPublishers Australia Pty Limited
ABN 36 009 913 517
harpercollins.com.au

HarperCollinsPublishers
Level 13, 201 Elizabeth Street, Sydney NSW 2000, Australia
Unit D1, 63 Apollo Drive, Rosedale Auckland 0632, New Zealand
A 53, Sector 57, Noida, UP, India
1 London Bridge Street, London, SE1 9GF, United Kingdom
2 Bloor Street East, 20th floor, Toronto, Ontario M4W 1A8, Canada
195 Broadway, New York NY 10007, USA

National Library of Australia Cataloguing-in-Publication entry:
Little, Valli, author.
  Delicious: sizzle / Valli Little.
  ISBN: 978 0 7333 3363 7 (pbk.)
  Barbecuing.
  Frying.
641.76

Author photo by Damian Bennett
Photography by Brett Stevens, Ian Wallace, Jeremy Simons
Styling by David Morgan, Louise Pickford
Cover and internal design by Hazel Lam, HarperCollins Design Studio
Typesetting by Judi Rowe, Agave Creative Group
Colour reproduction by Graphic Print Group, Adelaide SA
Printed and bound in China by RR Donnelley

6 5 4 3   16 17 18 19